THE FAMILY CIRCUS

Family shenanigans have long provided enjoyment for people everywhere.

Once, everybody loved Andy Hardy!

Then, there was Henry Aldrich!

Now, by all odds the most popular and entertaining family of the '60s, the five little rascals (including dog) who, along with Mommy and Daddy, make up Bil Keane's hilarious cartoon feature, THE FAMILY CIRCUS.

THE FAMILY CIRCUS

Bil Keane

A FAWCETT GOLD MEDAL BOOK

FAWCETT PUBLICATIONS, INC., GREENWICH, CONN.

MEMBER OF AMERICAN BOOK PUBLISHERS COUNCIL, INC.

A Fawcett Gold Medal Book published by arrangement with The Register and Tribune Syndicate, Inc.

"I said, DO YOU HAVE ANY CHILDREN?"

"It's all right, Jeffy — the doctor asked her to do that."

"I don't WANNA be a bad guy! I'm a GOOD guy!"

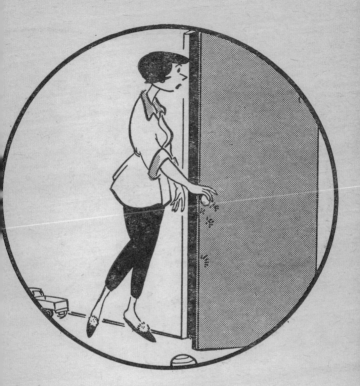

"We're asleep!"

"Mommy, what time is it when the big hand
is on a dot and the little hand is on a line?"

"Mommy, why did you just kiss that man
on television?"

"Is this mine or ours?"

"FORE!"

"Whose birthday is coming up?
Mommy and Daddy are spelling their talk!"

"I'm sorry, we do not bronze blankets."

"If you really want to see something funny,
let's go watch Daddy wake up from HIS nap."

"Is this seat taken?"

"It has craters, just like the moon!"

"But I CAN'T take a bath!
Billy and Jeffy used up all the bubbly stuff!"

"I can't find the toothpaste!"

"Don's Barber Shop? Prepare for emergency!"

"We're letting more flies in
so we can kill them for you."

"So this is where your Follow the Leader game was heading!"

"...And a large bag of lollipops."

"Now—you were saying?"

"Mommy! Where we going?
Barfy just jumped into the car!"

"But you said we could each bring
ONE THING to play with!"

**"It's a lucky thing PJ's still in diapers
while he's learning to walk—he needs the padding."**

"What's PJ crying for?
I'm the one who got hurt!"

"I promise I'll play with her every day
if you'll let me keep her!"

"When you were young,
your name was Thelma, wasn't it Mommy?"

"Kissing's over!"

"This must be a busy night for baby sitters—
you're the fifth one Mommy called."

"My goodness!
Look at those DARLING little handprints!"

"Why didn't we get out at the third floor, Mommy?
It looked pretty good to me!"

"Aw, come on Daddy—what ELSE would you like
for Christmas besides a raise?"

**"HO-HO-HO, neighbors!
It's midnight and here comes Santa Claus!"**

"If Santa Claus made this at the North Pole,
why did he write 'Made in Japan' on it?"

"Quick! Let's go watch Mommy! She said if anybody
stopped in today, she'd fly up the chimney!"

"...And when you see the Easter Bunny,
tell HIM to bring us..."

"Santa WAVED at ME!"

"Jeffy and Dolly licked all the envelopes for you
and I licked all the stamps."

"You're right, Mommy, that's 'zactly who it was!"

"You have to hold your mouth like this —
the way Daddy does."

"... And the daddy bear said, 'Somebody's been
sitting in my porridge and I think
it was Red Riding Hood's grandmother'..."

"Mommy told me to hold them
'cause she's on the phone."

"I'm trying to remember where I hid my scissors
so the children wouldn't get them."

"I need the cardboard for a project."

"Daddy's lucky! He gets all the mail!"

"There's a big new doggy across the street
and I don't think he knows us."

"Oh, you're quite welcome to what's left in the can,
Kate. Jeffy's bringing it over."

"Can we go see the dragons next?"

"Mommy, Jeffy's 'it' and can only count up to five.
Will you help him count to a hundred?"

"Mommy! Jeffy and I leaned an old board up
against the fence and made our own sliding board!"

**"Better get out of here, Barfy!
I think Daddy just found another one of your bones!"**

"Do you think the ice cream man would consider stopping in front of somebody else's house for a change?"

**"This is fun! I wish our washin' machine
would break down every week!"**

"Mommy says pos'tively no. You ask her next."

"May I have a cookie, Mommy?"

"Jeffy's looking for his cookie."

"Make Billy and Dolly stop looking at me."

"My teacher must really like me—
she put my desk right up next to hers!"

"Boy! Do I have homework!
I have to color all these balls!"

"It's my handprint in plaster. Which living room wall
are you going to hang it on?"

"It says 'The entire contents
of this envelope only $2.50!' "

"We'd better find out where Billy sits —
he's bound to ask 'Did you see my desk?'"

"Everybody comfy?"

"Daddy's playing that game
where it's HIS turn all the time."

"Daddy, will you watch me so I don't cheat?"

"My mother says if you want me to come
to your party, I have to bring home an invitation
or your mother has to phone her."

"Look at the prize I won!
Mrs. Sellers said to save it 'til I got home."

"I don't want to use the feather duster —
nobody can hear me working."

"I shook it out for you, Mommy!"

"I made them myself and
Mommy didn't have to do a THING!"

"We like it best when you're ironing or mending
'cause that's when you turn on TV."

"Mommy! It won't shut off!
Which way do I turn it? Help me, Mommy!"

"Mommy! This drawer won't close!"

"Mommy, you missed one of the squares!"

"That's not something to eat—it's Mommy's ironing!"

"In you go PJ — that's a good baby."

"Don't chew your fingers — you'll spoil your dinner!"

"ALL gone!"

"Mommy! Jeffy's eating the icing!"

"And no more arguments about who's getting the biggest dessert."

"Mommy's getting out all the mending—
Grandma must be coming for a visit!"

"Mommy hid our banjo and drum and toy piano.
Don't you and Granddad LIKE music?"

"Gee, Grandma! We didn't know you
knew how to change babies!"

"After Granddad plays with us for a little while,
why does he always go in and take a nap?"

"We're still too close to the driveway.
Grandma won't drive her car in till
we're over in the middle of the lawn."

**"Poor Grandma—there aren't any kids
living around here for her to play with."**

"Why can't we eat our 'zert FIRST—
while we're still hungry?"

"Mine is the peanut butter and jelly sandwich."

"Half for you and half for me! Mommy said!"

"The Wilmots were throwing all this good stuff away."

"My shoes are back at the lake, but it's okay
'cause I know 'zactly where I left them!"

"It was the best movie I ever saw!
We had popcorn and sodas and candy and..."

"Look! PJ's milk turned into cottage cheese!"

"It's okay, Daddy—Mommy spilled it this time!"

"Aw, Mommy—'in a minute' always takes too long."

"Were the pillow's 'jamas dirty?"

MOTHER'S
LITTLE
HELPER
KIT

"Is it okay to play on this part now, Daddy?"

"Are you going to put away
YOUR toys, too, Mommy?"

"But you only told us not to sit on the ARMS"

**"Don't take those crusts, Daddy!
That's the birds' breakfast!"**

"It'll be easier for you to tie my shoes when I grow up to be a man 'cause my laces will be longer."

"I don't think they were very hungry,
Mommy—they all flew away."

"It's a salesman, Mommy—should we
tell him you're not home?"

"Will your mommy scold you when you get home?"

"You ate the whole cake! I made it
for dessert for everybody!"

"See what PJ learned from you?"

"Hurry, Mommy! I think Daddy's getting dizzy!"

"What do you mean, 'where's PJ?'
he's RIGHT THERE!"

"Mommy, are we supposed to let you
sleep THIS morning or TOMORROW morning?"

"I stepped on a crack and Billy said
I broke your back!"

"No use crying—Mommy can't hear us from here!"

"Can I come in now? My eyes are cold!"

**"Why aren't they black like
Daddy cooks them in the summertime?"**

"May I sample five?"

"Did we do a good job of pasting in the stamps?"

"Wow! Look at that neat red light flashing
on the roof of the car behind us!"

"Poor Barfy. Other dogs only have fleas."

"A week till we go on vacation and the children next door have the measles!"

"Could the nose drops wait till I'm off the phone?"